Look for More Titles by Cassandra Chandler

The Blades of Janus
PACK

The Department of Homeworld Security (novellas)
Gray Card
Resident Alien

Seconds (short stories)
"Second Sight"
"Second Skin"

CRAFTING A WRITER'S LIFE: Building a Foundation

Coming Soon

The Department of Homeworld Security (novellas)
Business or Pleasure

The Summer Park Psychics
WANDERING SOUL
WHISPERING HEARTS
LINGERING TOUCH

Crafting a Writer's Life:

Building a Foundation

Cassandra Chandler

Copyright Page

First eBook edition: November 2016
First print edition: April 2017
cassandra-chandler.com
P.O. Box 91
Mission, Kansas 66201

Introductions are Important

When I started out, I had no idea what was involved in building a writing career beyond "write well". I worked on that part of the equation for over a decade before sending out the piece that landed my first traditional contract. What I've learned along the way could fill... well, this small book in your hands.

This book is short on purpose. Your writing time is valuable, and I'm honored that you're using some of it to read this. I want to share my knowledge as quickly and briefly as possible so that you can get back to the page. To that end, I'll share my experiences with learning about plotting, writing, and editing a book, as well as the insight I've attained into what can be involved on the business end of things.

Not every technique will work for everyone, and what works for one project might not work for another. I think it's good to try new things, especially if I find myself getting stuck in my writing. But feel free to disregard anything you read here that you don't think will work for you or your own creative processes.

Please also keep in mind that I'm not a doctor or a lawyer—nothing in this book is meant to give legal or medical advice. I'm just a writer sharing my experiences so far on my own path to building a writing career.

After reading this book, I hope you'll be closer to building a writing career that meets your needs and helps you to fulfill your dream of crafting your own writer's life. In the end, only you can craft the life that works best for you and make the decisions that will lead you there.

We need to answer an important question before we even get started, though. Here it is.

Why do you write?

It's easier to daydream. You don't need a computer or a notebook. You don't have to spend hours on end thinking through plots and wondering about structure and form. Why are we writers going to all this effort with our craft?

I think most of us write because we want to read the stories in our mind. We want to experience our stories in a tangible form, to share them with the world, or just with our own bookshelves—virtual or otherwise. And the only way to do that is to get them down on paper (so to speak).

This book encapsulates much of what I've learned so far about the craft and the business of writing. That's why I say this isn't just a book about how to write—this is a book about how to be a writer.

Let's get started.

Part One — Writing as an Art

Chapter One—Building Your Real-World Skill Sets

Being able to communicate through the written word should not be confused with being a writer. Many people can write. Not everyone considers themselves a writer—and with good reason.

Writing is an art form. There's magic in weaving stories. A certain amount of talent is involved, a great deal of skill, and an epic amount of hard work. Bringing a story into the world takes effort.

I think certain skills are fundamental to being a writer. I call them a writer's real world skill sets. They may sound simple, but they can be difficult to develop. I consider time and energy spent building them up as an investment in my writing ability.

Here's an overview of what I find to be the most vital practical skills in the art of crafting a writer's life:

Becoming an Analytical Reader
Learning to Type Quickly and Accurately
Capturing Ideas
Cultivating Flow
Maintaining a Sense of Accomplishment
Time Management
Self-Mastery
Boundaries

Becoming an Analytical Reader

The first step in becoming a successful writer is learning how to read. But wait a minute. You're reading this now—obviously you already know how to read.

This is similar to the difference between being able to communicate through the written word and being able to write stories. Reading *analytically* isn't just about understanding words. It's about seeing the form, structure, and choices that went into creating a particular story.

I used to be one of those readers who would be surprised by twists and turns right up to the end of a book, enjoying the ride the story presented and not thinking overmuch about the construction behind the words.

When I started focusing on how stories were put together, I began to notice things—the seams and cracks where the story was pieced together. I saw the intention behind the writer's words, which sometimes made it harder to enjoy the stories they were telling me.

The more I learn and the more I practice being an analytical reader, the harder it is for other writers to surprise me. I believe it's a worthwhile exchange for being able to craft better stories myself. It's still a sacrifice.

When I'm reading a book critically, I keep myself apart from the story so that I can analyze it. Here are the things I watch for while reading to improve my writing craftsmanship.

Were there any times when I was thrown out of the story? This can be caused by characters being inconsistent with what the writer has already set up, or the writer might contradict themselves or introduce continuity errors. If the hero's pet cat ran off in the previous chapter, it would be confusing for it to suddenly jump onto his lap with no explanation and no reaction from the hero.

An even worse issue would be if I ever became bored with the story. I may be able to forgive a writer who overlooks a few continuity issues, but if I get bored, I'm probably going to put the book down and not come back to it.

Reading analytically, I always try to figure out how the writer lost my attention. Did they stop the action so they could go into a sub-plot that didn't seem to matter to the rest of the story (or to me)? Did it feel like the writer was telling me things that the characters or setting could have communicated?

I make a note of every time I want to put a book down and why. Whenever I'm writing, I take extra care to avoid those pitfalls.

I look for the good as well. What story elements have me on the edge of my seat? What delights me and makes me want to keep reading?

Early on, I completed an exercise where I thought about the books I most enjoy reading. I figured out my favorite story elements among them and found the common threads. This exercise wasn't just fun, it also taught me about what sort of writer I wanted to be. The same things that delight me as a reader delight me as a writer. Writing a book can take months or even years. The first reader I need to keep glued to the pages is me. If I ever start to get stuck or bored, I know I'm veering away from what I love about stories. Knowing what I love about stories helps me to get back on track.

Learning to Type Quickly and Accurately

Being able to type quickly and accurately can be a great boon for a writer. I find that when I'm really immersed in my story, I'm barely aware of typing the words. If I used two fingers to hunt-and-peck each word on a keyboard, it would hamper my creative flow.

Some writers find that taking their time with typing helps their creative process, or they prefer to write on paper, editing their work when they type it in. Whatever their preference, it's still very likely that they'll have to type in their work eventually (unless they can hire someone to do so for them).

Building the skill to type quickly means having a *choice*. After cultivating my typing skills, I can either go slowly, letting the ideas percolate as I write, or get out the scenes that are burning through my mind as quickly as possible.

Capturing Ideas

All stories start as ideas, which are fleeting. It's important to me to be able to capture them quickly. Having multiple methods for getting down my thoughts is essential.

I almost always have a notebook and something to write with. The great thing about notebooks is that I can either write a few words to trigger my memory or actually write out longer scenes, bits of dialogue, and plot points when I have the time or inclination. Those few times when I've been caught without a notebook, I've been known to write notes on napkins, receipts—any paper that's handy.

Another great way to capture ideas is with an audio recording. I used to leave myself voicemail when I didn't have anything handy to write on.

I also think it's important to pay attention to when my ideas usually come to me. I try to make sure I'll be ready when inspiration strikes. I keep a journal by my bedside for late-night inspiration. Sometimes, all it takes is a few keywords to help me remember my thought. My bedside journal is also useful for writing down dreams that might be good fodder for stories later. By being prepared, I'm rewarded by having fewer ideas slip through my fingers.

There's a balance to documenting ideas and writing the actual stories, though. If I let myself get bogged down trying to capture every idea I have in careful detail, I won't have enough time to actually write anything.

Capturing every idea that comes to me isn't possible anyway. Life is busy, and sometimes I just can't get away to jot something down. If I don't remember the idea later, I don't let myself worry about it. I know I'll have more ideas, and if that one was important, my subconscious will churn it out again—possibly in an even better form.

Cultivating Flow

For a long time, I had a set schedule and a space in my home that was dedicated to my writing. I had special notebooks I would write in, and even pens that I had assigned to specific projects. I only wrote when I had huge blocks of time available and zero distractions.

What I discovered about having these rituals and routines for me personally was…I was actually less productive. *A lot* less productive.

If I couldn't find my pen, I couldn't get into my writing groove. I would waste time trying to find the specific notebook I had assigned to a writing project. Or I'd even skip writing sessions because I didn't feel inspired and was waiting for my muse to come to me.

I was learning during this time. Figuring out what kind of writer I am and developing the skills I needed to reach the writer's life I wanted to build—integrated with all the other aspects of my existence.

Since then, I've specifically trained myself not to rely on any external triggers to make my writing happen. I write at the kitchen table, on the bathroom floor, and even every once in a while at my writing desk. I write by hand when I need to, but try to type as much as possible—because that's what works for me. I may write for five minutes or five hours.

I never know when my writing time will be torpedoed, or when my writing space will be taken over for other activities. Such is my life, and I love my life. So I've trained myself to be able to write whenever, wherever I can. It wasn't easy and it took a long time, but it was one of the best investments I made in developing my writing skill sets.

Being able to stop a piece at a moment's notice and pick it up again quickly is very important, as well. I doubt I'll ever sit down and write an entire work in one sitting (unless it's really, really short). I see this skill as being able to put a mental bookmark in my story—like hitting the pause button.

If I only have a few moments to wrap up a writing session, I'll write a few keywords to trigger my memory the next time I sit down. All along the way during a project, I keep notes on what's happening in the story and with the characters so that I don't lose track of anything. While I need to devote some of my writing time to keeping up with those notes, I find they help me deepen my stories and look at things from different angles. Again, it's a worthwhile investment.

The most important aspect for me of cultivating the skill of writing anywhere, anytime is that I don't make any part of my writing into a ritual. There aren't specific things I need to do or use to write. I can sit down—or even stand—and write something in a notebook, make a voice memo, or type some dialogue in a quick email I send to myself.

Like most people, I have certain periods of time when I'm most productive. I figured mine out by writing at different times of the day and seeing when my word count was higher or lower, and looking for patterns. Knowing my patterns, I try to set up my writing times in those windows—but I'm careful not to *rely* on them. Being flexible and adaptable is key in my writing practice, and greatly boosts my productivity.

By training myself to write anywhere and anytime, it doesn't matter if my schedule suddenly changes and I lose my evening or morning writing sessions. I can shift it to whatever writing time I have available.

Maintaining a Sense of Accomplishment

Thinking about the actual act of writing is often a block for me. If I imagine myself sitting down and typing away for the hours, days, weeks, months it takes to write a book, I'll find other things to do. Things that give me an immediate sense of accomplishment.

I might clean out a closet or play a level of a video game. This can make me feel great in that moment, but there's often the sense of, "but I wanted to make progress on my writing" lurking in the background.

That's why I write out what I want to accomplish in my writing each day. I sit down at the very beginning of a project and make notes of not just what I want to do, but when I want to do it. I may decide I'm going to write a chapter a day. For a novella project, that's only fifteen-hundred words. For a novel, it's closer to three thousand.

If I let myself stop to think about the magnitude of the project—how long it will be till I have that sense of "I did it"—I won't even start. By marking my progress and letting myself feel the invigoration of accomplishing each step on the path toward a completed book, I keep myself motivated to carry on.

My particular process involves careful outlining. I make an initial outline and save it in a safe location. Then I make a version that I call my working outline. As I write, I move sections from the working outline into my draft. I flesh out the sections, transforming them into the actual manuscript.

Watching my word count grow while my working outline shrinks is a huge reward for me and gives me a great feeling of accomplishment.

That can help me keep going on days when it's hard to face the screen.

When a feeling of accomplishment isn't quite enough to keep me motivated, I turn to a reward system. At first, my rewards were things like pretty notebooks or special pens. But then I found that I would put off writing if I didn't have that particular notebook available. I thought about special meals out to celebrate accomplishments, but that can become expensive and unhealthy.

I decided that I wanted my rewards to feed my writing career. All I had to do was change my perspective on a few things.

Toward the end of writing a book, I can now keep myself motivated with the reward of, "as soon as it's done, I get to read it!" And when I finish edits on an indie title, I get to design the cover.

I might make a new background wallpaper for my computer, create a playlist of favorite songs that get me in the mood to write, or go for a long walk. In this way, my rewards are helping me to achieve all of my goals—a healthy, balanced writer's life.

The biggest reward for me is the act of writing itself. There's nothing like the feeling of having finished a work and seeing it in its completed form. Each story that I pick out of my mind and put down in a concrete form makes room for more stories to come into being. That's the biggest perk of all.

Most of the writers I've met have more than one story in them. While working on getting out the first book, they might think that's it—but a certain magic often happens after it's done. Suddenly they have another idea. Then another and another. I've seen it happen over and over with writers just starting out on their paths.

I've always had stories filling my mind. I use the pressure of all those stories waiting to be written to keep going. There's *always* another project waiting in the wings. It's the best motivator for me to keep showing up at the page every day.

As an added boost to keep myself on track, I try to never let myself start a new manuscript until I have a finished first draft for the current one. I still let myself write notes about the other projects, and even snippets of scenes or dialogue. But I don't want to write too much of them or I lose the chance for more motivators when it's their turn to be written. If there's a scene that's particularly gripping for me in a book, that's my reward for writing all the parts that lead up to it.

It can be rough. There's so much temptation to work on more than one story at a time. But this is how I write—and *finish*—as much as I do.

I finish projects in stages. There's the first draft, then editing, then prepping for publishing. I try to leave gaps of time between each stage. Giving my first drafts time on the shelf can be an important part of creating an excellent work. I might schedule some down time while the piece sits, where I recharge my creative energy, or I may start another project. I'm always happiest when I have something waiting for edits in the wings and something I'm writing that's new.

Some writers will have a system of working on more than one project at a time. When they get stuck on one project, they jump to a different one. Or they might write new material in the mornings and edit another piece in the afternoons. There are many systems for getting the words down, and all of them are valid.

Time Management

Another essential skill for my writing is time management. There are so many distractions that can lure me away from my writing time.

Some activities feed my writing, giving me inspiration and deepening my connection to others and the world around me. Others are time sinks, where I lose hours or even days and am left feeling that I've wasted time.

Periodically, I take a few minutes to write out all of my commitments. Health, family, work, community. I have to eat and sleep. My loved ones need care and attention. And, of course, I need to take care of myself as well. How much time do I want to give to all of these important aspects of my life?

When I wrote everything out, it initially seemed like there was no time left for writing. But I just needed to learn to budget my time and make room for writing in my life. I found that I had friends who were also interested in writing. We set up times to hang out and write or have discussions about what we were learning and what we hoped to achieve.

Making a conscious decision about how much time I would give to my writing is what helped me to actually find the time to write.

Self-Mastery

Of course, if I can't get myself to actually sit down and write, I have a problem. The books won't write themselves. I know that if I want to get better at writing, I need to work on it, practice it, think about it. I need to *write*.

Self-mastery is another vital skill for my writing, and really, it's what this chapter is all about. Learning more about myself—as a person and a writer—can help me identify the patterns that support or detract from my writing.

Often when I sit down to write, I'll hop on social media sites just to check on them "real quick". If I'm not careful, I can lose an entire writing session during these "quick checks". It's a pattern I keep a close eye on. I can also become distracted building web sites and blogging.

Building relationships on social media can be important, both for connecting with readers and with other writers. And having a web site and blog can also be very helpful for a writing career. But if I spend all my writing time working on those things, when will I write my books?

My main tool for keeping myself sitting (and writing) in my writer's chair is to continually focus on what I want to achieve and why I'm writing in the first place. It's not enough for me to make up entertaining stories in my head. I want to be able to share them with people in a tangible form that has value. Publishing books and making them available for sale pushes me to create my best works.

Sometimes, I can use the sense of accomplishment that I mentioned earlier as incentive to get writing. If I'm daunted by my word count goal, or procrastinating for whatever reason, I tell myself to put aside whatever is distracting me and write fifty words. Only fifty.

Once I get those few words out, I usually find myself motivated to write more. And if I stick with it long enough, I lose myself in the story —which is one of the best feelings I've ever had as a writer.

Even if I stall after those fifty words, by making the effort I'm telling myself, "My writing is important. I'm giving this time to my writing." My word count might not climb on those days, but my subconscious knows what I want it to be working on in the background.

Boundaries

My time is valuable, as is my energy and attention. I don't give them away lightly.

When I first dedicated myself to writing, it was sometimes hard for others to understand why I found it necessary to sit alone writing when I could have been hanging out with them. Even now, while I'm writing, people call or approach me and want to chat and seem confused when I turn them away.

What I'm doing is important. My writing is important.

That doesn't mean the people I love aren't important. I'm sure to give them time, energy, and focus to maintain those relationships. Setting boundaries around my writing time just means that I'm taking care of myself as well—giving myself the gift of recognizing that this is an important aspect of my being.

As much as possible, I surround myself with people who understand this. It's been incredibly helpful in supporting my writing practice.

For those people in my life who don't quite understand how important writing is to me, I need to have strong, healthy boundaries. If I've set a goal or have a deadline, I need to be able to request the time and space needed to get it done.

To help my loved ones feel…well, loved, I've given thought to how I want to handle potentially negative interactions. I'm a writer, so I wrote a script for kindly setting boundaries with people who request my writing time.

"I'm working on an important project right now, but could we meet up or call at X time and day?" Or, "I have an appointment that I can't miss. I'm available at X time and day, though."

Setting up another time to talk lets them know they're important to me, and proposing the time lets them know that my time is important, too.

One of the hardest lessons for me to learn in building my own writing career is that if I don't take my work seriously—and treat it accordingly—no one else will.

Sometimes I can be my own distracting force. I might sit down to write and think, "Oh, I need to do the dishes", or "I haven't talked to so-and-so for too long". It's also important that I don't let *myself* intrude on my writing time.

When I start to come up with excuses or distractions, I think about all the stories I want to write, then realize I don't have time to procrastinate. I remind myself that my writing is important and that I deserve this time to spend honing my craft and delving into my stories.

If you are a writer in your heart, I think putting off writing is ultimately self-destructive. I know I'm a better version of me if I give myself time to write. And that helps everyone in my life!

Chapter Two—First Drafts

There are many ways to get to a completed first draft. I'll be talking about the system that works best for me in this chapter. I'll also include a few other techniques I've tried or heard about along the way. Please keep in mind that with creative systems, there really is no right or wrong technique. There are only different paths.

When I started studying the craft of writing, I kept thinking I would figure out a single system that worked for my creative process. What I discovered was that different projects actually developed better through different methods.

For a large project that would take months to write, I needed extremely detailed outlines. I knew I'd be doing lots of starting and stopping, and had to keep track of where the story was going.

The smaller projects didn't require as much detail. There wasn't as much to keep track of, and they came together fast enough for me to remember more of what I wanted to do with them. I still jotted down notes, but those outlines were much more skeletal than for the bigger projects.

There are certain universal aspects that I found applied to every project, though. I needed to think up an idea and have it develop enough that it could hold my creative attention—and my readers' interest when completed. From the idea, I needed to do the actual work of getting a first draft down in a completed form. After that, some amount of edits or even a complete rewrite would be involved.

I've never heard of anyone sitting down to write a first draft and having it come out perfect. Knowing that I'll be editing my pieces gives me a certain amount of freedom in the first draft. If I'm not sure a scene will fit in with the finished version, but it sounds like fun to write and will keep my creative wheels spinning, I go ahead and write it.

Even though I often cut those scenes, I still learn more about the world, characters, or plot by writing them. That makes the story stronger. It's also writing practice, which makes me a stronger writer. They can sometimes make great bonus web content, too.

I let myself be a bit self-indulgent with the first draft, while keeping it as close to the finished story I plan to publish as I can make it. I've found that if I start a manuscript expecting it to come out perfect immediately, I'm putting too much pressure on myself—pressure that could block off my creativity and make it harder to actually write anything.

While writing my first draft, it also helps me if I tell my inner critic to remain silent. This can be hard. I find that taking a respectful stance with my inner critic works better for me than yelling at her. I want my critic on my side—during edits.

If I explain to myself that the first draft just needs to be written and finished, and remind myself that I will need that inner analytical voice during edits, I find it very balancing and helpful. I'm not telling my inner critic "No", I'm telling her "Not now".

Writing the first draft as quickly as possible is another must for me. I know this isn't the case for everyone. Some writers like to pore over every word and scene, letting the words unfold in their mind's eye. Their first drafts may be longer, more detailed, and closer to their final version.

My first drafts need speed. It's easier for me to keep my inner critic at bay if she knows that her turn will come soon. Plus, it helps me to keep the story straight in my head. I usually try to get the actions, reactions, and interactions down first, knowing I can go back and flesh out details and descriptions during editing.

Even with an outline, it's hard for me to remember every detail of an 80,000-plus word novel over a long period of time. When I write quickly, I don't have to spend as much time reminding myself of those details. I'd rather spend my writing time actually writing than reading through my notes.

I also find that I get into a groove more often when I write quickly. There's no time to doubt, second-guess, or attempt to rework my original plan. When I'm focused on getting a first draft done quickly, I usually hit my word count goals. That gives me the feeling of accomplishment I use to fuel more writing. It's a self-renewing source of motivation that has served me very well.

In this chapter, I'm primarily going to be describing my system for creating first drafts quickly using outlines. Using an outline doesn't mean that I never come up with ideas on the fly. My outlines are a framework to keep me on the path and help me write the story that I intend to. While actually writing the book, I'm still often surprised by the characters, and if a more compelling plotline emerges, I absolutely follow it.

At this point in my writing development, my outlines usually capture the story well enough that I don't deviate from them too much. It's especially important for me to stay on track because I'm writing multiple series, each with their own story arcs. I'll be writing in these worlds for years, and I want to make sure I'm keeping everything straight in my mind (and books). To do that, I use outlines, notes, and a series overview document. It may seem like a lot of extra work, but I think it makes my books stronger.

Here's an overview of what I consider to be the most important aspects of writing a solid first draft:

Series vs. Single Title
Characters—The Heart of the Story
Plot—It All Revolves Around the Characters
Pacing—Keeping the Reader's Attention
Setting and World Building

Series vs. Single Title

One of the most important decisions to make when starting a first draft is whether or not it will be part of a series or a single title. There are benefits to both.

A single title is exactly that. One story, one book. By the end of the book, I've tied up all of the plotlines in a neat bow and my readers and I are free to go on with our lives.

A series is usually more complex. For a series, I deliberately introduce elements that are *not* tied up in a single novel. I may have sub-plots or character arcs that aren't resolved for several books. At the same time, I need to make sure that there's enough resolution in each individual book for my readers to feel satisfied—and yet want to read more. It's a balancing act.

Writing single titles could sound appealing compared to writing a series. If I were writing contemporary stories set in worlds that my readers are intimately familiar with, single title books could work well for me. But in the case of speculative fiction or even historical fiction—worlds and societies my readers aren't familiar with—I'm looking at a lot of work for each title. I'll need to teach my readers about these worlds. And in the case of speculative fiction, I'll need to *create* them.

As a reader, if an author introduces characters that intrigue me, I want to know more about them. If they introduce a world that captivates me, I *really* want to learn more about it. And if they do both, I'm going to want more, more, more. That's why, overall, I prefer to both read and write series.

Writing a series means more work with checking consistency and continuity. I usually want each individual title to stand alone as well as being part of the greater whole, which means I need to re-explain the world and pertinent events to my readers in each book. But at the same time, I can also explore my worlds more thoroughly, immerse my readers in them, and discover things that I might miss in a single story.

With each book I write in a series, I give my readers more information about the world and the people within it. I can show them glimpses of characters they've already met and let my readers see how they're doing. Personally, I love that. When I care about the characters in a book, I want to know more about them. I feel that even more strongly for the stories I write myself. Series give me an opportunity to get to know them better.

Characters—The Heart of the Story

If a reader doesn't care about my characters, they most likely won't care about my story. There's no getting around this. I think readers need to see characters they can relate to—even a little bit—or they're not going to feel connected to the story. They need to be able to see at least some part of themselves reflected back in the characters' thoughts, words, actions, and circumstances, even if they're only thinking, "If I was in a similar circumstance, I might become like this character, too."

The reader doesn't have to *like* my characters, but I think they need to be able to empathize with them on some level. And if my readers *do* like my characters, they're more likely to stick with the story and see it through. When readers care about the characters, they'll want to know what happens to their favorites, whether it's the protagonist, supporting cast, or even the villain.

Protagonists usually need to be the most likeable characters in the book. It's possible to write a book—a *good* book—with an unlikeable protagonist, but much more difficult to keep readers engaged. Even if the reader can understand why the protagonist has an unlikeable personality (meaning the reader can sympathize with the character) they're still not as likely to be cheering for them or engaged with the story.

It also helps me to give my characters agency—the power to make choices that affect their circumstances. If a character is forced to perform an act of kindness, it won't have the same effect as when they freely choose to do so. I think my protagonists are more sympathetic if their actions come about through free will.

I try to connect my readers with my characters as quickly as possible in my stories—to engage them from the start. I want readers to be emotionally invested in every character I write, whether they want to see the character succeed or fail. To connect readers to the characters, I try to show them doing something brave or great or kind. I want readers to see my characters at their best, before I drag the characters through the worst experiences I can dredge up for them.

If there's important character history that my readers need to know to understand the protagonists, I share that so readers can understand where the character's personality came from and why the character is making the choices they make. I also do my best to reveal the character's traits and background through dialogue, internal monologue, and action. This is how I avoid the trap of telling my readers things I should be showing them.

A character might make lots of jokes, but with an underlying tension in how I describe his voice and body language that makes my readers wonder what he's trying to mask with his humor. Or she might present a tough exterior with her words and actions, but her thoughts betray her loneliness and fear about her life circumstances. These are all ways of establishing a connection between the characters and readers, and that connection is what will keep readers up past their bedtime, turning the pages to make sure the characters they've come to care about will be okay.

Even if my characters are extremely likeable, readers will get bored pretty quickly if I don't give anyone agency. By giving my characters agency, I keep them at the center of events. Their actions and choices drive the story. This is especially important for my protagonists. If the supporting characters are the ones creating all of the real change, I need to give some thought as to whether I've selected the right protagonist for the book.

While the protagonist's choices are feeding into the external plot, their internal struggle can enhance the events of the story. I can make the book even more exciting by making the external plot have a direct impact on what the characters have at stake personally.

It's great if the heroine is able to save everyone by repairing the ship that crashed on a deserted island. It's *amazing* if she does it while dealing with memories of her father being lost at sea and the near-paralyzing fear that her own children will be left wondering what happened to her for the rest of their lives if she fails.

See the difference?

I write books with high emotional stakes. I want my readers to cry with my characters, laugh with them, fear for them, and fall in love along with them.

To craft characters that have enough emotional substance for my readers to latch on to, I give most of them what I call a Traumatic Life Experience, or TLE. This is where the character's fundamental personality traits originated—what they're inwardly struggling with in the story. It might be one specific event that shaped (or warped) their perception of the world. It might be a problem they have with the world at large—something that resonates with them deeply and causes them emotional turmoil.

The TLE directly feeds their internal development throughout the book, and is a big part of their personal stakes. Whatever horrible thing happened to them in their life, the story I'm telling is their chance to overcome it, move past it, or just learn how to live with it and still be happy.

I write romances, so my protagonists need to have their "Happily Ever After" (HEA) ending. If I was writing a different genre, I could have the TLE destroy my characters instead of showing them overcome it. But that kind of story…isn't my thing.

Often I'll give my secondary characters and villains a TLE to flesh out their personalities, too. I may even show their TLE happening on the page, or give some characters more than one. When writing a series, these pivotal events can provide wonderful material to come up with new stories.

I may give readers a glimpse of a supporting character's TLE in an earlier book, but then wait until that character's story—where they're the main character—to show the resolution. And along the way, their TLE might even get worse, until my readers can't wait to see the character overcome it.

I believe all of my characters deserve my time and attention. The energy I invest in them by thinking through things that may not show up on the page still feeds into the story. I might never delve into the motivation behind my villain's nefarious plan, but if I've worked it out in my head, my readers will feel it. The work I've done in the background will seep into my words and make my book stronger.

Supporting characters can develop enough to need their own story. When writing a series, I'm always watching for characters who I think will become heroes or heroines of later books. They're not always supporters of the protagonist when they're introduced—they may be a lesser form of antagonist, or even a villain. I can have characters start out with a rivalry that becomes a strong friendship or unexpected alliance. Or put in the opposite—friends who become adversaries or rivals. Having a variety of dynamics enriches my stories.

The relationships between all of my characters are often a deciding factor in whether I can keep my readers' interest. People are fascinated by relationships and want to see how they'll play out. Will friendships withstand the strain of conflicting family obligations? Will estranged loved ones forge a new bond amid the external struggles they face together? Relationships can be key to a story winning over readers, no matter the genre.

Readers may even develop a kind kind of relationship with my characters if I give them enough to connect to. If I have a protagonist who moves through the world on their own and never really connects with anyone else, it can be hard for readers to connect to them as well.

Plot—It All Revolves Around the Characters

Once I've started laying the groundwork for the complex web of relationships my characters will have, I still need something to happen to them. This is where the plot comes in, and I'm often actually working with quite a few of them.

I'll have the main plotline—which is usually composed of the external events that act upon my characters. Then there's the internal plotline, where the characters are working through their own story arcs, processing their TLE, working through relationship dynamics, overcoming their personal demons, etc. I'll also probably have one or more sub-plots for my book, plus I might have a series arc to maintain.

Creating a good story is like weaving a tapestry. There are quite a few threads to keep track of when putting it all together.

As a romance writer, the relationship between the two main characters has to have as much or more importance as any other plotline. I like my plots to be meaty, with plenty for my readers to latch on to. I make sure that each protagonist has plenty going on internally as well, to keep my readers' attention.

In most of my books, I'll have the main external plotline, the romance arc for the main characters, their internal character arc plotlines and any sub-plots associated with those, any other sub-plots going on in the books, plus the series arc.

It can be a little complex.

I find that writing out a summary of each plotline helps me to keep things straight in my story (and my head). I also sometimes make spreadsheets to track timelines so I can see when plot points are revealed and what characters who aren't actually in the scenes I write are doing. This is even more important if I'm writing multiple books with overlapping action (scenes that take place from more than one point of view in different books).

If I were writing mystery, the plot would center around whatever question the main character is trying to answer. I would have a strong internal plotline for the protagonist as well, and work in relationships to give my readers more avenues to connect with the story and characters. I'd probably weave in a sub-plot or two, either as false leads or as ways to enrich my readers' experience.

There's usually a character-driven question that readers are wondering about at the center of every story. Will the protagonist find peace with their relationship with their sibling/spouse/parent/child? Will they solve the murder/find true love/slay the dragon/take over the kingdom? Will they decide to continue living the status quo, or make a massive shift in their life, sending ripples (or shockwaves) through the lives of people around them that they care about?

A strong external plotline can keep my characters moving forward, toward the answers to those questions. I just need to remember that if my readers aren't curious about what will happen next, they aren't involved in the story.

The external plot starts as something happening *around* my protagonists. As they're swept up into the plot—or even better, as they boldly march into it—things start happening *to* my protagonists. And all the while, they have things going on *within* themselves.

I find that stories have even more impact if the protagonist wants something independently of trying to resolve the main plotline— something that's tied in with the main story. Maybe the main plot is that the protagonist is part of a team trying to save humanity by building space stations with clean air and water. They have years to get the work done—but the protagonist's partner is suffering from a quickly escalating respiratory illness. He's fighting to get the project done early to give her the best chance of survival.

Giving my protagonists goals makes my stories have a stronger impact with readers. If the protagonists *want* something, my readers can cheer them along on their journey.

This is where stakes come in. What is at stake in the story, both externally for the world, and internally for the characters? What does each character want? What will happen to them, to the other characters, and to their world if they don't get it? Answering these questions not only helps me to connect my story to my readers, it helps me come up with the plot itself. Whatever my character wants, the antagonist wants the opposite.

Maybe the protagonist wants to provide food for their community, but the forces of nature—a valid form of antagonist—are working against her. Maybe he's trying to discover what happened to his sister after she was recruited into a secret organization, but they want to keep their secrets to themselves. When I figure out what my characters want and how their relationships both impact and are impacted by their desires, I've usually found my plot.

What if the supporting characters want things that are at odds with the protagonist's goals? A grandparent wants to travel now that they're retired, but their son was counting on having help in raising his own children. They both love each other and want everyone to be happy. How do they find a resolution where everyone's needs are fulfilled? Is it even possible?

The stakes need to be high and personal to make the kind of impact with my readers that I'm looking for. I need to maintain the stakes at an intense level to keep my readers' interest. Is the world in danger? Someone the character loves? Their livelihood or life?

There may be lulls in the story, where I let my readers catch their breath a bit. But I still want them to be wondering what's going to happen next. Otherwise, they might put my book down and forget about it.

Pacing—Keeping the Reader's Attention

A story can have fascinating characters in compelling situations, and still leave readers cold. Unfurling the events of a story at a snail's pace will most likely bore the reader. Bombarding them with so much information and action that their mind shuts down can make them run away. In either case, the story will fall flat.

Pacing is how quickly—or slowly—events take place in the story, and it's a very important element to pay attention to while writing. If plot is about weaving the tapestry of the story, pacing is about finding the story's breath.

There are a few key components that are universal to controlling pace in any genre.

The pacing of a story can actually be controlled through the prose—not just through the characters' actions and the plot. Sentence and paragraph structure, word choice, and chapter breaks are all part of pacing. Writers can even communicate the tone of a scene or event with these tools.

During a lull in the story, I might have a character wax poetic about something, thinking or speaking in long sentences, bigger paragraphs, and polysyllabic words. When I'm explaining things or painting a picture of my world, I'm okay with writing longer phrases.

In an intense action scene, I want clipped sentences. Tight paragraphs. Short words. Action.

I want my readers' minds to tear through those scenes, reading as fast as events are taking place. This is where I want to leave them breathless.

In a scene that's more laid back, possibly sensual, or involving mind games, I want my readers to immerse themselves in what's going on. I might use more eloquent expressions, choosing words that have texture, crafting sentences that make readers stop and reflect on what's going on.

Emotionally intense scenes can be handled either way or land in between. But I try to make it a conscious choice so I remain aware of the pacing always. I might have a character expound on every horrible thing the protagonist has ever done, tormenting them with their failures. Or I can let my readers simmer with the characters in the white space on the page—dwelling on what *isn't* said.

Every book I write will be filled with pivotal moments for my characters—and my readers. I don't want to treat each of them in the same manner. Variety in sentence structure can help readers stay engaged by having them mentally switch gears.

Pacing happens at every level of a story. In every word.

Chapter breaks are one of the most powerful pacing tools. I try to make most chapter breaks suspenseful so my readers want to go on, but I also need to give them a chance to mentally catch their breath. They're like commercial breaks in TV shows. I want my readers to think, "Whew", and then almost immediately, "I want to know more", and turn the page.

Cliffhangers can be a fine way to end a chapter, but if they're overused, the can exhaust the reader or leave them frustrated. I want my readers to feel like they can go get a drink or a snack while reading —I want them to be comfortable. But I also try to structure my story so that they can't wait to come back to the page and see what happens next.

It's worth noting here that some genres have longer or shorter chapters than others. Figuring this out is an important part of the research that goes into planning and writing a book. Are readers of this genre used to reading longer, denser prose? Or are they looking for a quick read that's zingy and they can speed through? The work I did when thinking about my favorite authors and genres helped here.

Pacing is a way writers can maintain tension in stories, and tension is one of the most important reasons that readers keep reading. A well-formed plot can also result in catharsis—an emotional release for the reader. I want my readers to become all wound up, then vent all that tension at the end of the book, right along with the characters. Hopefully, some of the readers' real-world tension will exit along with it.

Tension is hard to keep up, and pacing is vital to maintain it. I believe that pacing is one of the most important aspects in the crafting of my stories. As such, we're getting to the heart of my system here. Again, this is what has worked best for me so far and goes into what I think is one of the strongest story structures. Every writer will find their own paths and build the system that works best for them.

I'm a big fan of stories written in three acts. There are tons of books out there with slight variations on this story structure that dig deeply into this topic. For the sake of brevity, I'm going to give a quick version of my personal take on it.

Act one introduces the world and most of the main characters (even if I just mention everyone briefly). There may be overt or veiled references to the antagonist or what will become the main conflict of the story.

At the end of the first act, I set up the rest of the story by having the first Really Big Thing happen. This is where the heroine learns that the hero is an alien, or the hero finds out that the mystery he wants to solve will very likely get him killed.

The Really Big Thing leads us into act two by posing a question—what is the protagonist going to do about the situation? Usually, there are two options. Move forward, or walk away.

My book could be really short if the protagonist chooses to walk away. Or that could be the meat of my second act—they try to get away from the action, but it's everywhere.

The second act is where I get to explore my characters, their world, and the events surrounding them. This is also the act where writers most often start to ramble. I'm very careful that what I'm writing here actually serves the story and doesn't detract from it. I lay the groundwork for later plot reveals, maybe give my readers a peek at the main antagonist.

Will the protagonist have to eventually climb a mountain to retrieve an artifact that's vital to the plot? I'll have the mountain in the background at some point, and let the protagonist think about his paralyzing fear of heights.

Around the middle of the story, everything will seem to be going pretty well for the protagonist. They're feeling good about their choice to follow this path, and it looks like everything's going to work—OH

NO EVERYTHING IS CRASHING DOWN AROUND THEM. I have twists and turns in store for my readers, and want them to know they need to hold on to their seats (and keep turning those pages). From the happy middle point onward, things need to go downhill fast for my protagonist. Nothing is going as planned. Allies are deserting—or worse, betraying—the cause. Relationships are strained. Resources vanish. The protagonist wonders what she was thinking at the beginning of act two when she decided to move forward on this path.

Now, again, I write romances. My protagonists never give up. They're determined to get to their HEA, and not afraid to work for it. Of course, internally, they may think they're doomed, but they put on a strong front for the people counting on them, and have faith that everyone will rally. This doesn't mean I don't put my protagonists through the wringer. I want my readers to have strong feelings for my characters. If I go too easy on them, my readers won't be as invested in the outcome.

At the end of the second act, the protagonist is well and truly screwed. They (and my readers) have no idea of how to get themselves out of the bind they're in.

And then, as the third act begins, the protagonist has an epiphany. It might be triggered by a secondary character giving them yet another pep talk. It might be from a rival trying to beat them down—or using antagonism to lift them back up to being a worthy opponent. It might be the villain crossing a line that dare not be crossed.

The result will be the same. The protagonist picks herself up, internalizes all of the experiences she's had through the book, and realizes what she needs to do. This is where the hero painstakingly pulls himself onto the cliff from where he fell off that scary mountain, no longer afraid of heights—or at least master of that fear. This is when she knows that she has to fight to achieve the life she longed for from the beginning—the motivating force behind her decision at the start of the second act.

We've come full circle with the characters, and they're ready to face the main antagonist one last time. There's a final climactic scene, and then the resolution. If it's a happy-ending story, the protagonist wins and the antagonist is vanquished (even if the series boss is still lurking in the background). If it's a tragic story…maybe not so much.

As the writer, it's my job to wrap things up with a neat little bow so that my readers can let out a contented sigh (or shudder), smile (or count their blessings), and then hopefully go out and buy my other books because they had so much fun with this one.

That doesn't sound so bad, right? It's an outline, but there's tons of flexibility in it. There's one more thing, though. I haven't talked about the math yet. Yes, math.

The three act story structure gives me the form. Doing the math gives me the dimensions of the project, and I've found it absolutely vital to how I control my pacing.

If I take up over half the book just setting up the world (first act objectives), that doesn't leave much room for building the conflict. And if three-quarters of the book consists of fight scenes between the protagonist and the villain, where will I find the space to build their personalities and give my readers something to connect with on a deep level?

This is why I outline.

I start by making a list of everything that I want to happen in the book. I try to put them in a chronological order that makes sense. Then I look for key moments, highlights, really big events or revelations that will blow my readers' minds and have them eager for more. That's where I find my pacing points.

At this point, I'm ready to do the math.

Most three-act stories follow a pattern. I'm a big fan of this pattern, as are most readers, even if they're not aware it exists. The three-act story structure has been around for a really long time.

I aim to have my first act take up about one fourth of the book. I give myself more wiggle room here than anyplace else in my pacing and word counts, but I try not to go much under one fourth and not much over one third of the book.

The second act takes up about half of the book. Adding that to the first act, that takes us to about three-fourths of the way through. The mid-point happens in here, where everything seems great, but things are about to come crashing down around the protagonist. And that takes place as close to the middle of the book as I can make it.

The final act—and again, here I give myself a bit more wiggle room —is the remaining one fourth of the book. Act three can be a little shorter than one fourth of my word count, but I try not to make it longer. That can cause my story to drag.

Before I sit down to write a project, I usually have an idea of how long I want it to be. I did research on the standard word counts for the different genres I was writing in, and how publishing independently differs from preparing pieces for traditional publishing houses. Most publishing companies or agents will state an idea of their accepted word counts in their submission guidelines.

Once I know how long a piece will be, I can do the math. If I'm writing a full-length novel, I'm usually aiming for 80,000 words. That makes everything easy. The first act is 20,000 words, the second act is around 40,000 words, and the third act is about another 20,000. That puts my key moments at around 20,000 (end of act one), 40,000 (the middle) and 60,000 (end of act 2).

Doing the math is a kind of magic for pacing. It keeps me on track and tells me if I'm dragging the story or rushing things along too fast.

For my short, snappy, Scifi novellas, I aim for 20,000 words total. That puts my key pacing points at around 5,000, 10,000, and 15,000. If I check my word count and see that I'm in the 7,000s, but I haven't reached the end of act one, something is seriously wrong. I'm rambling or using too many words or trying to set up too much too soon. Conversely, if I'm at 7,000, and I've already reached the "everything's great" midpoint and am well into the, "the world is burning all around us" descent, I'm going to need to go back and see what I skipped over.

Knowing standard word counts for the type of story I'm writing helps me provide my readers with an experience they find familiar and enjoyable. It stops me from going on and on in scenes that won't necessarily hold my readers' attention and keeps me from glossing over scenes that I want to pump up for all they're worth.

If I think I'm going to be diverging from my readers' expectations in the structure of my story, I think it's a good idea to let them know in advance. If I were to use a shorter form when writing an epic High Fantasy, I might alienate readers who are expecting a longer book. Or if I ever planned for a Cozy Mystery to hold my readers' attention for 200,000 words, they might also want to know that in advance.

This is important enough to me that I'll sometimes put my word counts in the synopsis for my indie titles—to be sure my readers know what they're getting before buying the title. I want my readers to be happy and keep coming back for more.

Setting and World Building

The genre I'm writing in can directly impact the importance of the story's setting. For a story set during modern times and in an environment familiar to my readers, the setting might not take up too much space on the page. In a Scifi epic, with space battles and strange aliens from completely new planets, setting will play a vital role.

It's important that I give some thought to how important setting will be for my stories. Am I just setting the scene as a backdrop for the characters? Or will the setting itself become a kind of character in my narrative?

Sometimes, even a familiar setting can take on extra importance. If I'm writing a series set in a small town, I'll want to describe locations in greater detail—perhaps focusing on an ice cream shop in one title and the Town Hall in another. Revealing more about the town can feel like revealing more and more backstory for a supporting character.

For space epics, fantasy worlds, historical fiction, or anything my reader isn't familiar with, I need to pay close attention to my setting and do some serious world building. World building is a catch-all phrase for the work a writer does in developing and then communicating things like the environment, customs, and even the laws of physics that govern their story's setting.

In a society with sorcerers performing true feats of magic, I need to know how, when, and why the magic works. Is it more potent on a full moon? Is it based on sacrifice? Is it common or rare? I find that with magic, it's a good idea to associate a cost for the characters. If someone can come in and solve the protagonist's problems with a wave of a magic wand, it can be hard for me to raise the stakes in my story.

If my book is set on a spaceship, does it have artificial gravity? I don't have to actually figure out and explain how to create an artificial gravity field (unless I'm writing hard Scifi, and want to have a system that people already understand, like using centripetal force in a spinning space station). It's enough that I set up rules such as, "the field works normally in hyperspace, but not near the gravity field of a star."

The important thing for me here is to be consistent. If the artificial gravity on my ship is disrupted by proximity to a star in one book, that needs to happen in all of them. And if I explain the situation by saying the gravity field of the star interacted negatively with the ship's systems, my characters will probably have similar issues next to a black hole or even a massive planet. I shouldn't break my own rules once I've set them up.

All of that world building work can lead to a terrible temptation, though—the dreaded information dump. This is the urge to tell the reader everything I came up with for the background of my story…as if it's part of the story.

That's not the way it works in my writing process. The world building I do feeds into my story, but shouldn't dominate it. I don't want my fiction books to feel like travel guides. I'm careful to only tell my readers what they need to know, when they need to know it. If necessary, I remind them of what I've already told them later on in the story.

All the world building work I do is important though. My readers will *feel* the backstory, even if I don't put it on the page. Spending time on world building enriches my setting, descriptions, and characters, and makes my story that much stronger. And if I really, truly must share my world building work with my readers, it can make great bonus web content.

Setting can convey a mood or strengthen the theme of my books. Maybe my character gets some terrible news, then walks out into a bright and sunny day, where everyone is cheerily going about their lives as if the protagonist's world hasn't fundamentally shifted. Maybe there's a heat wave that's been making everyone have short fuses, and the rain only comes to break the heat after a murder, washing away the evidence as well as cooling the tempers that lay behind the crime.

I have to be careful how I describe the setting as well as with the choices I make surrounding it. The "show-don't-tell" rule is in full force here. This frequently used expression doesn't mean that I should never straight-out tell my readers something. I just try to have the information come through a character—either in their thoughts, words, or actions. Giving readers any information needs to happen naturally for me.

If a character starts thinking about the history of telephones while working with her personal trainer, there needs to be a reason. Most people don't think about technology while they're working out, and this kind of situation could feel inorganic to the reader. Now, if the character happens to be an engineer who has a big presentation later that day revealing a new holographic projection phone she's designed, I could probably make that work. The important thing is to make the character's thoughts feel natural to my readers.

My setting description needs to be the same. People don't usually think things like, "The sky on Signus 5 is purple and the clouds are made up of flying ferrets." Instead, I would have the character think, "The sky was paler than usual—more lavender than anything else. A tight cluster of flying ferrets was dipping and diving in amazing acrobatic displays. Whoever thought to genetically engineer the bizarre creatures was a lunatic."

When I pay attention to how I give my readers information, I think it helps the story flow more organically and keeps my readers' attention better. It has to make sense for the characters to be thinking, saying, and doing what they are.

Chapter Three—Editing

Finishing a first draft is an amazing accomplishment. Many writers are so excited to have a finished story, with a beginning, a middle, and an end, that they immediately send it to a publisher or agent. They may even self-publish it right away.

This…might be a mistake.

First drafts are sometimes called rough drafts. They've been given this name for a reason. Ideas rarely come out fully formed or perfect.

I am a firm believer that *every* story can benefit from editing. Even ones that are already published could probably be improved—a word choice here and there, boosting a character's motivation or the descriptive prose used for the setting. When I re-read my own books, I always find ways I could have written them better (after all, I've gathered more experience since I wrote them).

First drafts almost always need several rounds of thorough edits. Honing editing skills can take a writer from being talented to being *skilled*. With patience and hard work, a first draft can be polished until it shines.

Here's what I'm going to talk about in this chapter:

When to Begin Edits
A Word About Grammar
Choose Your Style
Strengthening Your Prose
Edit as if It's Someone Else's Work
A Word About Genre
Pacing Yourself

When to Begin Edits

There are different schools of thought on how and when the editing process should begin. Some people say to get the first draft out and immediately shelve it for as long as possible. Others dive right in and start editing, and don't stop until they have something that's ready for the world. Some people even edit as they write their first drafts.

My system falls somewhere in between and changes based on the circumstances I find myself in. For instance, I rarely let myself edit while I'm writing a first draft. An exception might be if I was working against a submissions deadline. I might want to be sure that the first pages or chapters absolutely shine and let myself edit the beginning of the work before sending it in to make the deadline, but only if I knew I'd have time to finish the manuscript while what I'd submitted was being reviewed.

For the most part, I write my first drafts as quickly as possible and don't allow myself to edit anything. By the time I finish it, I have a few ideas of areas that need to be strengthened. I also have a list of things that I need to go back and change. They might be as simple as, "the heroine is now left-handed" or as complex as, "make the hero more assertive".

I don't consider my first draft ready to be shelved until I've made these corrections. While I put them in, I go ahead and do a first editing pass to fix errors that pop out at me and to make the prose a bit shinier. At that point, I consider myself to have a first draft, and put it on the shelf for later edits.

I want to be clear that this is the system that works for *me*— evolving over more than a decade of work dedicated to honing my craft. The first drafts I wrote when I was just starting out are... unsalvageable. Going through extensive edits will not help them. I'm confident they will all need to be completely rewritten. I'm okay with this, because the act of writing them—and finishing these first drafts— taught me so much.

I didn't start doing in depth editing on first drafts until I started producing drafts that felt sturdy enough to stand up to them. I just kept writing first drafts, learning about structure, pacing, characterization— focusing on *writing*, rather than editing.

When I was finally ready to learn how to edit   to make a first draft ready to share with the world—I had to move entire chapters to radically different locations in the story. It was an incredible amount of work. But the end result was absolutely worth it—and became my first traditionally published novel, *Wandering Soul.*

Applying myself to learning how to edit took my writing craft to a whole new level. It made the initial drafts and even my outlines stronger.

Some writers wait until they have their content exactly where they want it before they really edit their prose thoroughly looking for grammatical mistakes and the like—often called "line edits". The concern is that they may spend time editing paragraphs or even chapters that they eventually cut from their final manuscript.

I don't follow this mindset. To me, no time spent editing is wasted. Even if I pore over a chapter and then cut it later, I gained valuable experience practicing my editing skills. Every time I edit a paragraph, a chapter, an entire manuscript, I become a better editor—which makes my writing stronger.

The main thing I need to watch out for with editing is making sure that I'm ready to let the project go when it's time. Since I'm a better editor with every pass over a manuscript, that means I can edit the book again and make improvements. It's a cycle that can go on forever, really. I have to make sure I don't get stuck on any one piece or work on it for too long.

One of my goals when I set out to improve my writing craft was to be able to write well quickly. After years of focused effort, my first drafts come out pretty clean. Part of that is because I *do* conduct line edits on my drafts, even while I'm still tweaking the content. And after so many finished works and a ton of practice with editing, the bulk of my content is now pretty much where it needs to be even in the first draft. I've edited quite a few pages that are sitting in trim bins, but the extra experience made me a stronger writer.

A Word About Grammar

Because writing is a creative art, writers can choose to ignore certain rules of grammar... sometimes. Overall, however, I try to stick with the rules as much as possible. My main concern is for my readers to easily understand what I'm trying to say, helping them enjoy their experience reading my book.

There are a few things I've learned along the way that have improved my writing. The first is learning when to use a hyphen "-" and when to use an em dash "—". Hyphens are a component of some words, like "ever-changing". They're also used to connect words that make up a single idea, like "hot-and-cold". I can do a lot artistically with a hyphen.

An em dash is longer than a hyphen, and can be used in the place of parentheses or colons. I find it gives a sense of a stronger pause than a comma—without going so far as to place the end of the thought in a new sentence. Which I sometimes do.

It's also used to show when someone is cut off in the middle of a—
See?

This brings us to another frequent problem-participle—the ellipsis. An ellipsis is another way of showing a pause, but it's a longer, gentler pause. This can be a moment when the character's voice trails off...or their mind shies away from a painful thought. Ellipsis is written with three—and only three—periods.

Using multiple punctuation marks together, like "?!" or "!!", isn't generally done. The idea is that emphasis is better conveyed through word choice and setting up the scene. I've even heard that writers should limit their *single* exclamation points to one or two per manuscript. This is a real challenge for me, and I always seem to end up deleting quite a few exclamation points from my first drafts.

Again, this is all my experience. From what I've heard, agents or editors might consider manuscripts that break these particular rules to look less professional.

I will not go into the Oxford Comma debate. It is too contentious.

I will say that in almost every case, writers should have a comma before each "but". I'm sure I've seen correct examples of sentences that use "but" without the comma, but those are very rare cases.

I will absolutely share my opinion of paragraph structure. I feel very strongly about this.

When a new character begins to speak or takes action, I believe that needs to be in a fresh paragraph. If I have two different people talking and taking action in a single paragraph, I might confuse my reader. Breaking up paragraphs when new characters speak or act is vital for reader comprehension. We've been trained to expect a new paragraph when there's a new speaker. I think it makes my prose stronger to follow this important rule.

Choose Your Style

Readers are generally happier if a writer is consistent within their manuscript. I like to stay consistent across all of my works. To keep track of the decisions I've made on how to note certain things, I keep a style guide.

Indicating a possessive in a name that ends in "S"? Cass's choice is to add an apostrophe-"S" to the end. Other people leave off that extra "S".

How about writing letters? I note letters as capital and within quotation marks. "A", "B", "C", and so forth.

And I set internal quotes within dialogue apart with a single quotation mark or italics, depending on the situation. "I may have a character 'quote another character', or if it's a really emphatic quote, *it might be in italics.*"

Toward vs. towards? Toward. Always.

Strengthening Your Prose

As a writer, I believe it's my job to create prose that my readers can understand. There are a few key issues that I always watch out for. Any time a pronoun is confusing, I use the name instead. It can be a bit cumbersome if I have several people talking and doing things in the same scene, but I do my best to work that all out for my audience.

If I repeat the same word in a short amount of space, the repetition can be boring for my readers, or even throw them out of the story.

These repetitions are called "echoes", and I remove them wherever possible. English is a remarkably versatile language in this regard.

Some authors are against using a thesaurus to help in these cases, thinking they should only use common words. I do turn to the thesaurus, but try to stick with options that I think my readers will either know or be able to understand in the context of the sentence.

I also try to avoid using unnecessary words to convey my ideas. When I use extra words to control my pacing, that's one thing. But if I'm just rambling on about something, my readers have a higher chance of becoming confused or bored.

Some words are also seen as inherently weaker than others, or I might find that I use the same words too much throughout my works. I made a list, and do a check for those words in my final editing pass. If I notice too many instances of a particular word popping up throughout my manuscript—other than words like "the" and "of" and "a"—I try to edit some out. I sometimes will give myself a budget for a specific word, like being able to use "moment" once every ten pages instead of ten times in one page.

While using words to convey ideas to my readers, I'm careful to paint a scene that makes sense. The characters' *gazes* meet across a crowded dance floor, not their eyes. It's vague if I write, *Her hand moved closer to the key.* Was it still attached to her body? Can she remove it and control it mentally from across a room? Now I'm freaked out.

I also don't want to give my readers too much similar information too close together. I'm creating a mental picture for them, and I don't want to muddy it. *The alien hid* next *to the heather* behind *the barn* across *from the mill the government agents were investigating.* Too many positional references close together can be confusing.

Similarly, having actions stacked on top of each other can not only be confusing but downright impossible. I don't want my characters engaging in simultaneous action, which is when they do several conflicting things at once.

He managed to get the werewolf into a chokehold as he opened the door. I'm pretty sure getting a werewolf into a chokehold would take both hands. If the character is opening the door with his foot while getting the werewolf in a chokehold—which seems really unlikely—I need to go ahead and tell my readers that.

I also check that the character has enough time to do whatever I have planned for them. There's usually not enough time for the hero to give a long speech *and* run across the room to stop the villain from pressing the Evil Plan button if the villain is already standing right next to it.

Instead of always using dialogue tags like, "he said" or "she asked", I can mix things up by embedding action into my dialogue. I can have the dialogue be its own statement, then add a line of action showing what the character is doing while they're talking.

"Why would you want to do this?" you ask.

"Because I never want my readers to become bored with my stories." Cass leveled her gaze at the person holding this book. "Do you?"

Embedding action in dialogue can add drama and tension, and can certainly keep things interesting for my readers. Very, very, very occasionally, I'll use a dialogue tag other than "said" to add variety. I try to keep them straightforward when I do, like "he whispered" or "she growled".

If there's information that my readers need, I try to work it into dialogue while the characters are dealing with an emotionally gripping situation or taking some sort of dramatic action. This is another place where I'm careful to avoid the dreaded info-dump. I'm careful to only tell my readers what they need to know when and where they need to know it. This leaves their minds open enough to immerse themselves in the story I'm weaving for them.

Keeping the story interesting is the most important priority for me. I do my best to hunt out stagnant scenes, where characters are just sitting around or are talking or thinking about things that don't have a strong impact on their internal or external story arcs. I don't ever want my characters to be in a boring situation.

Edit as if It's Someone Else's Work

Editing is hard work. There's no getting around it. I need to polish my words, think through my scenes and dialogue, and above all, I need to cut material that doesn't work—even if it's a favorite scene, line, or character.

I chant these words quite a bit while editing: *Be. Merciless.*

It helps me to keep a trim bin. Instead of just deleting what I can't use in a piece, I save what I take out in a separate document. I never know when I'll write a piece where that particular descriptive passage, that snippet of dialogue, or even that beloved character will fit right in.

Reading my piece aloud—or better yet, having someone else read it to me—can help pinpoint problem areas. Where do I get confused? Where is the prose unclear or the wording repetitive?

I think it's important to know when to bring in other people, especially when first consciously working on improving as a writer. Even after training myself to find all of these issues in my work, I can still become so familiar with it that I overlook a simple mistake.

I've heard that it can be easier to find grammatical errors when reading a book backwards. I did this once. Only once. Not only did editing my book starting at the last sentence and working my way to the first seriously mess with my head, but I overlooked an important continuity issue.

Reading backwards, the scene showed a group of people talking, and then a character left the room. Thankfully, I did another read-through in the correct chronological order...and caught that I had written the character leaving the room *before* he was involved in the conversation.

Some writers have brains that can handle reading in reverse to check for grammar. I salute them! And I'll keep editing from the beginning.

A Word About Genre

While I'm going through edits, I keep my book's genre in mind. It can affect my choices and my readers' experience of the story.

In a world where magic is possible, saying that a character flew into the room can leave readers wondering...did they really fly? If I'm writing about flame-beings living in a star, they probably wouldn't say, "Burn!" when one of them gets the better of the other verbally. What would that word even mean to them?

Genre can affect word count, word choice, and even the structure of my prose. I always research what readers are expecting in a particular genre, and try to let them know in advance if I'm thwarting convention.

Pacing Yourself

Like it or not, I know I'll be making several editing passes before my story is ready for the world. During each pass, I'm careful not to try to do too much so I don't lose track of what I'm looking for. I always check for flow and grammar issues to make sure the prose sounds the way I want it to. And I make sure I have my notes handy for the things I need to fix with plot, pacing, and characterization.

Above all, I keep myself ready to let go of things I love. The first draft is for me. The one I publish after edits is for the world.

Chapter Four—Everything is Personal

When I'm writing my first draft, everything is personal. This is the draft I write for myself. Because of this, it can become more personal than I intend. During edits, I'm always watchful of how much of myself I leave in my book.

I never write about people I know. Or even places or events.

"But aren't you supposed to 'write what you know'?"

I don't think so.

There's a big difference between writing a place that I know and writing a *setting* that I know. Growing up, I played in a swamp quite a bit. I know what that specific kind of swamp is like. That doesn't mean that I took the actual swamp where I played and put it in my books.

I use my knowledge of what the environment of that swamp was like—sand, fennel, sphagnum moss in the trees—and use that to enrich my description for my readers. I may be writing about a place I've never been to, other planets, other worlds. It can help my readers if I ground the characters' experiences in what I know of reality.

The same goes for the people in my stories. I base my characters on archetypes—a collection of broad generalizations of human traits. There might be a woman who's totally focused on her career or a man whose sense of self-worth comes from how others perceive him.

As a writer, I'm uniquely positioned to explore the nature of human experience—even in the case of inhuman characters. I start from characterizations, and build up characters with the traits I want that fit the story and setting I'm developing.

I see part of my job as a writer to be making the places and people in my stories *feel* real to my readers without them actually *being* real. I'm not writing memoirs, I'm crafting stories. I put enough of my own personal truth into each book that my readers can feel it, but not so much that they can't see themselves and their own experiences reflected in the characters, the world, and the story.

Part Two — Writing as a Business

Chapter Five—Selling Your Work

Writing is an art form. Selling my work... That's a business. It helps me to remember this while I'm writing my books. I'm creating something that I plan to sell, and that will have an impact on some of my choices while writing.

I've talked to many writers who don't want to look at their craft this way. Some people think that grounding their work in the business side of being a writer will taint it or make them less of an artist.

I don't think that considering the business implications makes my work any less artistic. I certainly feel fulfilled when I finish a piece. And the best sense of artistic satisfaction I've ever had was holding one of my published books in my hands.

My outlook is that creating something from nothing is art. Being able to sell it—that's business.

When I started out, I had only the vaguest idea of how the business side of writing worked. Submit to a publisher—get chosen or not. If chosen, then my book would magically appear on bookshelves. If the book was rejected, I'd submit it elsewhere.

I've found that there is a great deal more to it than that. In this section, I'm going to cover everything that I wish I had known starting out, and share my experiences so far. Since I'm a hybrid author, I can give a glimpse into both the indie and the traditional publishing worlds.

Here's what I'm going to be taking about:

Royalties and Bank Accounts
Your Book is a Product
Creating a Final Product
Editing and Beta Readers (no, not your mom)
Taglines and Blurbs
To Summarize or Not To Summarize
Speed as Industry Standard

Royalties and Bank Accounts

I don't think I've ever heard a writer's group sitting around talking about where to keep their royalties, however I think it's an important enough topic to give some thought to. Some writers may decide to link their publishing funds to their everyday bank account. Others might open a new one to keep those funds separate.

Certain expenses can be involved in building a writing career— purchasing swag (promotional items intended to be given away to readers), guild memberships, convention costs, copyright registration fees. Maybe one writer will have a writing-specific credit card for this purpose to make tracking expenses easier when it's time to do taxes. Another may find that some guilds might only accept checks or that a publisher they're interested in working with only pays writers through a specific online venue.

These are important things to figure out. Only you can decide what's right for you and what you're comfortable with.

Your Book is a Product

I know, many of you are cringing at the thought, but it's true. If you plan to sell your book, it's a product that you are providing for people to buy. There's nothing wrong with this. Artists deserve to be paid for their work.

Let me say that again.

Artists deserve to be paid for their work.

It's true.

If an audience wants the experience of reading a book, it's okay that they need to pay for it. People pay to watch movies or TV shows. People pay to go to amusement parks. They buy pieces of art to decorate their environments. Why wouldn't they pay for books?

It takes an incredible amount of time, effort, and resources to write a book. If people are reading my book, I believe I deserve to be paid for it. This means that my book—the experience of reading my book—is a product that is available for sale.

This is a good thing.

Creating a Final Product

If I don't hunt out my typing errors, polish my work, and shore up my plot holes, it will hurt my book's ability to sell—and probably impact how my future books are received.

There are universal steps involved in creating a book that's ready for the shelves. We went over the steps in writing a book from an artistic side, but here they are again viewed from the business side of things.

First, I need an idea. Something that can catch my readers' interest. Of course, I need to write the story and get it down on paper (or electrons). After that, it's all about editing.

Editing and Beta Readers (no, not your mom)

I've already talked about the parts of editing I can do on my own and that familiarity with my prose makes me more likely to overlook errors. Eventually, I always want another pair of eyes on my work. This is one of the ways that a writing support group can be very helpful. If none of my writer friends can assist, I can hire an editor to assist me.

It's important to make sure that whoever I turn to knows what they're doing and is a good match for me as a writer—whether they're a hired professional, a writing colleague, or a friend.

When asking for feedback, I often remind myself that writing is an art. I don't want to blindly accept any input I receive about ways to strengthen my work.

There is no true right or wrong way to do things. There's just what's most generally accepted and, of course, the actual rules of grammar.

Having artistic freedom with my writing doesn't mean I can write incomprehensible manuscripts. If I'm writing to sell a book, my audience needs to understand what I'm talking about. Having others who can read my work and give me feedback is immensely helpful with this.

I searched for a writer's circle that both helped my craft and supported me emotionally during the ups and downs of building a writing career. Artists can struggle with all kinds of self-doubt.

Talking to others who are going through similar experiences can help me—especially when I hear myself encouraging them after they've expressed the same self-defeating sentiments I'm telling myself. I realize that I, too, am doing good work. That it's a worthwhile effort.

If you've made it this far in this book, honestly, that makes me think that you *need* to be a writer. It isn't a passing fantasy or a pipe dream. It's in your blood. In your heart. If you have a writer's soul, I believe it needs to be fed by putting words down on the page and crafting them into that thing which is at the root of our shared human experience—*a story.*

Find your people.

But be cautious. Writing can be a lonely enterprise. As much as I love sharing my work, I'm always extremely careful that the people I entrust with my work are deserving of that trust. It took me several tries before I found the right fit, but it was absolutely worth the time and effort to find my writers' group match.

A common way that writers help each other out is by reading each other's manuscripts and providing feedback on them. Most people use the term "beta readers" when talking about people who read their works and provide feedback. I think it's more complex than that.

"Beta readers" is a reference to testing that's done in software development. Before a new software package is deployed, it goes through a rigorous testing process (hopefully), where people try to find any errors (bugs) in the system. The beta test is usually the one right before the product goes on the market.

Drawing from that analogy, I consider a beta reader to be someone who reads my manuscript when I think it's one-hundred percent ready for the market. I've edited it myself, I've had other people help edit it, I've polished it till it gleams, and I think that it is ready for readers to buy.

My beta readers still usually find issues that I need to fix. That's why they're so important.

Some writers decide to share their story much earlier in the process. They may even share it as soon as they finish the first draft. This is an absolutely valid choice.

In software development, there's also something called an alpha test. Alpha testing goes on early in the development stage. The software is nowhere near perfect, and the people working on it are looking for early feedback. Does the display look good? What sort of glitches do the testers encounter? Does the overall functionality meet their expectations of what the final product will do?

I call sharing a rough draft or any snippets of a rough draft alpha testing.

If I have a character who seems to be coming across as too brash or arrogant, I might ask my writing circle to read a few early chapters and let me know if I'm being too critical of myself (and my character). If I'm afraid my world building isn't quite right or that my magic system makes no sense, I can run that past my writer friends. Every interaction surrounding writing can teach me new things about the craft.

Here's the catch, though. Once someone has read my work, they've already started becoming familiar with it, making them less likely to catch errors in later read-throughs. Because of this, I try not to ask the same people to be both alpha and beta readers for a given manuscript.

I consider my relationship with the person who's reading for me as well. My family is probably going to tell me that my work is great, even if it needs a lot of work. Close friends can feel the same way.

Another question I ask myself is whether the alpha/beta reader is familiar with my genre. High fantasy has a totally different feel than a snappy contemporary romance. Different characters and experiences are acceptable in different genres, and since I'm trying to market and sell my book, I—and my test readers—will need to be aware of this.

Before I agree to read for someone or have them read my work, I might ask them to make a list of possible trigger issues. I give them a list of my own as well, and add to it as I learn more about myself. The last thing I want to be reminded of when I walk into an alpha or beta reading experience is my own issues. I know this is the section about "writing as a business", but this is actually a very important consideration.

We all have our own issues—experiences that we bring to every story we read. As a beta reader, it won't matter if I'm reading the most amazing story ever, with incredible writing and compelling characters. If I'm constantly being triggered while reading it, I'm going to miss things.

No matter how I decide to proceed with alpha or beta readers—professionals I hire or qualified friends or colleagues willing to help—the following components of my book must be edited: content, character, plot, pacing, consistency, continuity, and form. I need to make sure the content resonates with readers, the characters are sympathetic enough to not turn them away, my plot is interesting, my pacing holds my readers' interest, I'm making sure my characters and world behave in a consistent way, that I don't contradict myself, and that my work is free from typographical errors.

The more I edit, the more practice I get, the easier it becomes. It's helped me develop what I call my writer's intuition, which guides me to the passages or character traits that need work. The more I write—and edit—the better my writing becomes.

Many writers want one final pass to make sure nothing was overlooked. This final pass is often called line edits. Line editing generally focuses on grammatical and typographical errors. Hopefully, by this point all of the plot holes and inconsistencies have been addressed, but after all the times I've reviewed my manuscript, it can be hard to notice little issues like a comma instead of a period. It can make my book even stronger to take it through this polishing step.

Taglines and Blurbs

Nowadays, writers need to take on more of the marketing aspects of publication. I don't know of any publishing houses that will do all the work of marketing my books for me. Whether I plan to independently (indie) publish a book or go with a traditional publisher, I think writing a tagline and blurb for each project is good practice.

The tagline is the one or two sentence slogan that gets readers' attention. It needs to be catchy and short. I like to come up with several taglines for each title, then pick the one I like best, maybe getting feedback from a few trusted people.

The blurb is also sometimes called the "back jacket copy". This is the text found on the back of a book—or next to the online product description for digital copies. Blurbs are meant to give readers an idea of what the story is about and make them want to buy it.

Writing the blurb for my books helps me think about my story in a different way. I'm not seeing it as a creator—I'm seeing it as a customer. Who is the main character? What is the main plotline? I can't give away too much, but need to give readers enough to intrigue them.

If I'm indie publishing my title, I'll need to either write or hire someone to write a blurb for my book. No matter what path I'm taking, I try to write at least one version myself. Even if I don't use what I write, it gives me a better idea of the key points of my story that might appeal to my audience.

Taglines and blurbs can also be used in queries to traditional publishers and agents. If I can hook them with these, that's a really good sign. It also shows them that I know more about the industry and can think about things from a marketing point of view.

To Summarize or Not To Summarize

Writing a summary of a story can seem like an exercise in futility. It's like writing the book all over again—but only in a few pages. Summaries are very useful, though. Agents and publishers don't have time to read every manuscript they receive. A well-written summary can keep me from getting lost in the slush pile (the publisher's pile of submissions).

If I'm going to be working with a cover artist, blurb writer, or marketing company on an indie title, I'll probably need to send them a summary, too. That one will most likely be much shorter than the one I use for an agent or publishing house.

I might also use a summary as a sort of outline when I'm first setting out to write a book. I'm just careful to update it before sending it to anyone for use with my final book, in case any elements of the story changed while I was writing it.

If someone stops to ask me what my book is about, I need to be able answer in one or two sentences. What if I end up in an elevator with my dream editor/agent/publisher? I'll want an awesome pitch that I can fit into a few seconds. Hopefully, that pitch will hook them and they'll want to know even more.

For each title, I try to make a summary that's a few seconds long, a minute or so long, and then maybe a few longer versions for if I really get their interest. In the end, I always have to summarize. Whether it's writing my own blurbs for indie titles or submitting a pitch or sending a draft of a blurb to my publisher or telling a reader about my book. It's worth the investment of time.

Speed as Industry Standard

The speed of publishing is faster than ever. There are so many books already available, and more being published at an amazing rate. In order to gain traction in such a saturated market, it helps to write quickly—as long as the quality of my books doesn't suffer for it.

Readers want stories. If they find one of my books and like it, they may look for more of my work. If they don't find any other titles by me, or there isn't anything new for them to read within a few months, they're more likely to move on to another author.

To help with the speed of my output, I make any necessary formatting settings to the document as I write. I usually know in advance if the title is meant to be indie published or I'll be submitting it to a traditional publishing house. If it's indie, I'll format the work for publication as I write. Words I want to emphasize will actually be in *italics* instead of underlined. On the other hand, if I plan to go traditional with the title, I'll check the submissions guidelines for the company or agent I'm sending it to, and format accordingly.

In all cases, I want to create professional-looking work. I go ahead and check my manuscript for dangling spaces at the beginning or end of paragraphs. I only use one space after each punctuation mark within a paragraph and clear any unnecessary tabs or weird formatting characters.

When an agent or publisher looks at my manuscript, I want them to see that I'm willing to work, I'm respectful of their time, and I know enough about the industry to take care of these issues, no matter how inconsequential they seem. And if I decide to indie publish the title, well, I'd have to do all of that eventually anyway.

Even though I'm aiming for quick output, I still do my best to leave my work on the shelf for at least a few weeks before doing the bulk of the editing work. I want the lingering afterimage of the manuscript to have a chance to fade from my brain so that I come to the manuscript with fresher eyes.

Part of my writer's speed is being practiced at setting a manuscript aside so I can work on whatever I need to for the deadlines I receive, and then diving right back into my ongoing project. Being able to change direction without losing momentum has been a challenging skill to develop, but a crucial one.

I may suddenly be called to do edits when I'm about to write the pivotal scene in my current rough draft in progress. Guest blog posts, special anthologies, edits for a contracted work—I need to be ready to switch gears at a moment's notice. The writing world moves *fast*. I need to be ready to embrace opportunities when they arise.

Chapter Six—My Publishing Experience So Far

As of this book's first publication, it's been a little under a year and a half since my first book came out. Most of my titles are published traditionally, and I have a few independent or indie titles (self-published).

There are myriad avenues to getting my work in readers' hands as an independent—or indie—author. With indie publishing, I can do as much or as little of the work as I want. There are companies that offer formatting services, editing, cover design, even distribution and marketing. Hiring out the work can be expensive, but it saves time and energy. Doing it myself is more difficult and time consuming, but I find it very gratifying.

Then there's the traditional route. Going traditional means submissions to agents and/or publishing houses, writing queries, and waiting for results. If my piece is accepted, it also means that I'll have a team of trained professionals working with me every step of the way, guiding me through the process, handling distribution, formatting, cover design, and helping me through edits.

Not all traditional publishing houses provide the same level of service for their authors. I've been extremely lucky so far. I've also researched every company I've submitted a piece to thoroughly—asking other authors about their experiences, checking web sites that have relevant information.

Working with a team means that we need to agree upon an end product. It's extremely important that I work with companies that will treat me and my books with respect.

I started out in traditional publishing, and found that I wanted a deeper understanding of everything that was involved in creating a book—from the initial idea to seeing it on the shelf. That was one reason among many that I decided to become a hybrid author.

Hybrid authors have some titles available through traditional publishing houses and some that they publish independently. I've learned so much from my indie pieces, and can use that experience to make my traditional titles even more successful. In this chapter, I'll share what I've learned about going traditional, indie, and hybrid.

Going Traditional

Research is a big part of being a writer. I need to learn about the world to better describe it. I need to observe human behavior and interactions. It makes my stories better. Research is also a big part of my writing career, no matter the route I'm taking to publish a work.

When I first had a book that I thought was ready for the world, I went online and found out everything I could about the publishers that had caught my interest. I looked at shelves at bookstores and searched for patterns in books that I liked. Were they from the same publishing house? That was a clue. I asked my writer friends what they thought and what sort of experiences they'd had.

After narrowing the list down, I did even more research. Did the publishing house have a blog? What sort of articles did they post? Did my books match their product line? Was my writing style one that I thought they would enjoy? How would my voice sound next to their other authors' in the chorus of their published titles?

That narrowed the list down more. Then I started looking for editors. What names kept coming up in writers whose works I enjoyed? Which editors made a good impression with writers at conventions? Did they have blogs? Other social media feeds? Seeing someone's online persona was a way to get a hint of what they might be like to work with.

When I sign a contract, I'll most likely be agreeing to work with that company for years. Things can change over that amount of time, but when first starting to work with a publishing house, it's so important to do the research, to see their track record, and make sure I'm signing up to work with people that I can respect and who will make the experience one I enjoy.

Going Indie

This book marks my fourth venture into indie waters, and I've already learned a lot from this part of the journey. Indie publishing gives me total creative control for each title. It also lets me experience every step of making a book.

I like designing my own covers and the process of formatting books for print and digitally. And it's great to see people enjoy a work that I made myself, from start to finish. It's a lot of work, but it can also be extremely rewarding.

I've worked hard to build a great support network for my writing. I have writer friends who are absolutely qualified to do everything from alpha reading to line editing. I have graphic artist friends for when I have questions about cover design. I have a marketing maven who understands more about how people think than I could ever comprehend. And I have professionals I can turn to and hire for help any step of the way.

When I was first venturing out into the indie world, I decided to learn a little bit at a time. I had built my infrastructure and created my product, but navigating the waters ahead required a great deal of care and caution. Once again, I was going to be signing contracts. Setting up accounts. Agreeing to Terms and Conditions. Learning the rules for formatting ebooks and print. But this time, I was the only one who would be responsible if something wasn't the way it needed to be.

I started with learning about making my own covers. Then I taught myself how to format ebooks. After I'd launched a few of those, I learned how to format books for print.

It's important to me that I get these things right—that the products I create for my readers are of consistently high quality. I'll say this again—if I don't take my writing seriously, no one else will. Taking the time and care to really study how indie publishing works is part of how I take my writing seriously.

I am a firm believer that writing is an act of faith. I'm having faith in myself that I can stick with the story all the way to the end. I believe in my ability to craft a book of high quality. I have faith that other people will want to buy and read it. Indie writing has been an even bigger act of faith for me. In the end, it's just me and my book. But holding that finished product, knowing that I made every bit of it—from the initial concept to the book in my hands—is one of the most rewarding writing experiences I've ever had.

Going Hybrid

There are several reasons that I decided to become a hybrid author. Aside from learning more about the various aspects of the publishing process, I also wanted to be able to put out some titles on my own timeline. Publishing some of my titles independently is extremely helpful in not overtaxing myself.

In traditional publishing, edits can come in when I'm not expecting them. Marketing opportunities might come up that I can't let pass me by. I could be plowing through my latest rough draft, and have to set it aside for a few weeks while I work on a contracted novel.

If I set aside an indie title to meet a contracted deadline, the only person I'm answering to is myself (as long as I haven't promised anything to my readers yet!). I can keep working toward all the series that I want to put out without negatively impacting my contracted work.

I'm still finding my way, but am extremely happy with how things are going and the progress I've made. Trying both paths to publishing and settling on becoming a hybrid author is what works for me right now. I'll keep assessing what works and doesn't work, so that I can adjust my path as necessary and keep producing works I (and my readers) love.

Chapter Seven—Nothing is Personal

When talking about writing as a business, nothing is personal. This can be hard to digest.

My work feels very personal. These are my books, and I've poured my time, energy, and heart into them. I've made sacrifices and worked hard to finish them and get them out in the world.

As a writer, I've spent weeks, months, or even years on my books. A reader will spend a few hours at most. I can't imagine them feeling the same sense of importance to my works. This was an important revelation for me—no one will ever care about my writing as much as I do. And that's a good thing. I want my readers to be entertained by my stories—not obsessed with them.

Not that *I* become obsessed with my stories...

Anyway, it can be difficult to maintain perspective when interacting with readers. In this chapter, I'll share some of the ways I create and maintain my professional boundaries, including:

Dealing with the Public
Visibility and Communication
Managing a Social Media Presence
Processing Reviews

Dealing with the Public

The person writers are in their everyday life is not necessarily the writer-self they present to the world. There are many reasons to keep parts of their life away from their writing career. It's up to each individual to decide what they're comfortable sharing.

I decided what and how much I was comfortable sharing early on. Once something is shared with the world, it's hard to take back—especially with the ubiquitous nature of technology. What I say online can follow me for my entire career. I try to be mindful of that always.

Some writers (including me) talk about specific hobbies they have.

They'll post pictures or write blog posts to connect with readers about those topics. Alternately, if there's a common theme that runs through their books or characters, they might talk about that as part of their writer persona. Maybe their characters love to bake or read or go for nature hikes. If so, the writer-self they present to the world might talk about those same topics. They might share recipes with readers, favorite books, or post pictures of nature settings. These patterns can create a way to connect with readers without giving them more information than they want or need about the writer's real life.

Some writers are more comfortable simply interacting with their readers without this buffer. They may decide to express whatever's on their mind and that their personal life is part of their writing career. It's up to each individual to decide what and how much they want to share.

Visibility and Communication

My readers won't be able to connect with me as a writer if they never hear from me. I also had to decide *how* I was going to communicate with them.

I consider having a web site to be a vital part of maintaining a writing career. My web site is where I make announcements about my books, where I blog, and where I help my readers connect with places where they can buy my books.

I personally have chosen to not sell anything directly from my web site, but instead have a dedicated page for each title, with a selection of buy links, the cover and blurb, and links to anything I think might encourage them to buy the book. I might include a short excerpt, links to good reviews, or awards the title has earned.

There are plenty of hosting sites that make building web sites easy. There are also lots of people who can be hired to design web sites.

The core components of my web site are my blog, a landing page for my books with sub-pages dedicated to each title, a newsletter signup and archive page, and an "About" page. I take care of building and maintaining my web site, and have tried several different formats. My readers seem to most enjoy seeing my blog front-and-center.

My blog is a chance to show readers what my writing style is like. It's not quite the same as my author's voice in my stories, but readers can still get a better feel for me as a writer through it. I can also work to draw in more readers by posting about interesting topics that are related to my books.

To build a blog following, the standard advice is to publish one new post a week—but more is better. They don't have to be anything fancy. I most often post a quick update about something writing-related, or some reflections about what's going on around me, or even just a picture with a few words.

Newsletters are another great way to keep in touch with readers—right in their inbox. There are many good newsletter management sites as well. Along with the signup link, I like to have archives of previous newsletters on my newsletter page. That way, readers can see what they're signing up for.

I took the steps involved in acquiring the domain name I wanted: cassandra-chandler.com. I was also able to set up an email address that I use specifically for my writing: author@cassandra-chandler.com.

Having this personalized online presence presents a more professional image to readers and the people I work with in the publishing industry.

Managing a Social Media Presence

Social media is a powerful tool for connecting with readers. For me, it is also one of the ultimate distractions from writing.

Learning how to balance my social media time is a challenge. It's fun to connect with other writers and interesting people. It's fantastic to talk to readers about my books. But in the end, if I don't have new books coming out, I'm not making the most of my time.

I do my best to set limits with myself so that I don't get caught up chatting with people online when I'm supposed to be writing my next piece. I'm also careful about the boundaries I set for myself right as I was starting out as a writer. My number one rule is that I never let myself vent on social media. I don't want negativity in my feeds.

I think it's a good idea for writers to give some thought to their own boundaries surrounding what they'll talk about on social media. If they're using the same social media sites to keep up with friends, relatives, and/or coworkers, *plus* their readers, they're probably going to face more of a challenge keeping up strong boundaries. This is part of why I was talking about creating a writing persona earlier.

Processing Reviews

Reviews are tricky ground as well. Whether good or bad, they can take writers on a roller coaster ride that can hamper their ability to write.

I do my best to remain emotionally detached from my reviews. Reviews are one person stating their opinion of a book I've written. If I couldn't detach myself emotionally from my reviews, I wouldn't read them. And I admit some are harder than others to keep at a distance.

I imagine walls and walls and walls of barriers between me and each review to help me keep emotional distance from them. I look for the good and consider the bad. I always look for patterns. What do the readers love about a piece? What do they hate? Is there a common thread that spans different books and/or series? These are important clues that can help me become stronger in my craft.

I'm also careful that I don't give reviews—or any feedback I receive about my writing—too much importance when I'm planning pieces or actually writing them. My books need to stay true to my voice and my vision for them. These are *my* stories, after all.

Part Three — Writing as a Calling

Chapter Eight—Why Do You Write?

When I started on this journey, one of the most important questions I asked myself was, why do I want to write? Did I just want my daydreams in a tangible form? Was I looking to share with like-minded people just for fun? Did I want to be able to tell those who ask that I've been published by a company who believes in my work? Was I interested in building a lasting career?

If I don't stop and really think about what I want, the only answers I'll get to these important questions will come from outside of me. From family and friends, colleagues, and even strangers. My vision of the future could be shaped by what I read, watch, and overhear—and that isn't what I want.

I actually sat down and wrote a writer's mission statement, including what I'm trying to accomplish with my writing. It taught me a lot about myself and shaped the path my craft needed to take.

Are you most interested in having your voice be heard? Changing perceptions? Providing an escape? Making people think? Championing a cause?

No one knows what you want—what you need from your life—and what you can uniquely contribute as well as *you* do. And the only way to know the right answers is to ask yourself, and really listen to how you feel. I think all writers should spend some time thinking about this, and write down their thoughts.

Life gets busy—especially when my writing picks up—and going back to these answers helps keep me on the right path, even when I'm adapting to changes.

Chapter Nine—Finding Balance

Writing is an important part of my life, but it's only one part of my life. I need to be sure I'm supporting my entire self, not just my writer self. It can be easy to get caught up in a piece and forget the rest of the world.

Time moves too quickly. Days or even weeks can pass before I realize it. I sometimes have to remind myself that there is a big world out there—a *real* world. One that needs my attention.

I have a tendency to lose all sense of time while I'm writing a story. I keep a planner with all my important dates in it, including my writing accomplishments and goals. Having the writing information right there with the rest of my personal deadlines helps me keep on top of the important parts of my life.

Writing is often a sedentary activity. It's hard to type or write while moving around. I try to incorporate as much exercise as I can into the process—pacing in a clear stretch of room while I read a book for edits, for example, and only pausing when I need to jot down a note.

But that isn't really enough for me to stay healthy. I need to plan meals. I need to get up and get moving. For me, yoga is an absolute necessity. I'm not the happy, productive, best version of myself without it. I make batch meals and store them in containers that are an appropriate size for my needs, whether it's a dinner portion to feed many or a lunch portion just for me.

It's important to me to remember to take care of the people in my life as well as myself and my writing. Sometimes, I ask writer friends to have our chats while going for a walk. This has the added benefit of keeping our relationships strong.

I firmly believe that those of us who are meant to be writers need to write every day. Even if it's just daydreaming about a storyline or imagining how one of our characters would react to a situation at the grocery store.

Figuring out what I need to be the best version of me, while still taking care of my loved ones is a key part of building a successful writer's life. I know I can find a way to be fulfilled as a writer and still maintain the rest of my life.

For me, writing isn't optional. It keeps me sane, strong, and stable, and makes me the best version of myself so that I can be there for myself and others.

I also remind myself to be ready to handle disappointment. It's hard to avoid on the path to becoming published. Whether it's a cover I'm making myself that just won't turn out exactly as I want, a negative review, or a discouraging lack of any—disappointment is part of what I need to learn to deal with.

Writers face rejection constantly. It might be in the form of an agent who passes on my work, a form letter from a publisher that isn't interested, or readers who don't connect with my work the way I want them to. I need to learn how to deal with disappointment and how to be patient.

And finally, to find balance, I work to keep hope alive. I want more people to discover my books and to love them. It's early in my career. I believe this will happen given time.

I liken crafting a writing career to building a house. With each book or series, I'm decorating a new room and making it inviting to readers. At first, the rooms will be mostly empty. I have to have faith that eventually these metaphorical rooms will be full of readers sitting in the comfortable chairs I've painstakingly created, looking at the pictures on the walls, and eating delicious imaginary sandwiches.

Building a writing career is a long game. It will continue to change and grow throughout my life, teaching me, inspiring me, and making my life fulfilled. I wouldn't have it any other way.

A Note for the Reader

What did you think? I'd love to hear from you through a review. If you'd prefer another way to connect, you can stop by my blog (www.cassandra-chandler.com), follow me on Twitter (@CassChandler) or Facebook (CassChandlerAuthor), or even send me some email at author@cassandra-chandler.com. You can also stay in touch by subscribing to my newsletter (www.cassandra-chandler.com/newsletter). There are many more adventures to come.

Thanks for reading!

About the Author

Cassandra Chandler has studied folklore and mythology for her entire life and been accused of taking fairy tales a bit too seriously. She sees the starry sky as a destination rather than a matte painting, though her primary residence is on Earth. Her romances range from sweet to scorching, set in extraordinary worlds and driven by characters searching for a deep and lasting love.

www.ingramcontent.com/pod-product-compliance
Lightning Source LLC
Chambersburg PA
CBHW050604280326
41933CB00011B/1976